A MIND MADE *Beautiful*

A gentle guide to owning and healing your mind

JENNA MACKENDER

BALBOA.PRESS
A DIVISION OF HAY HOUSE

Copyright © 2025 Jenna Mackender.

All rights reserved. No part of this book may be used or reproduced by any means, graphic, electronic, or mechanical, including photocopying, recording, taping or by any information storage retrieval system without the written permission of the author except in the case of brief quotations embodied in critical articles and reviews.

Balboa Press books may be ordered through booksellers or by contacting:

Balboa Press
A Division of Hay House
1663 Liberty Drive
Bloomington, IN 47403
www.balboapress.com
844-682-1282

Because of the dynamic nature of the Internet, any web addresses or links contained in this book may have changed since publication and may no longer be valid. The views expressed in this work are solely those of the author and do not necessarily reflect the views of the publisher, and the publisher hereby disclaims any responsibility for them.

The author of this book does not dispense medical advice or prescribe the use of any technique as a form of treatment for physical, emotional, or medical problems without the advice of a physician, either directly or indirectly. The intent of the author is only to offer information of a general nature to help you in your quest for emotional and spiritual well-being. In the event you use any of the information in this book for yourself, which is your constitutional right, the author and the publisher assume no responsibility for your actions.

Any people depicted in stock imagery provided by Getty Images are models, and such images are being used for illustrative purposes only. Certain stock imagery © Getty Images.

King James Version (KJV), public domain

The ESV® Bible (The Holy Bible, English Standard Version®). ESV® Text Edition: 2016. Copyright © 2001 by Crossway, a publishing ministry of Good News Publishers. The ESV® text has been reproduced in cooperation with and by permission of Good News Publishers.

Print information available on the last page.

ISBN: 979-8-7652-5795-1 (sc)
ISBN: 979-8-7652-5714-2 (e)

Balboa Press rev. date: 04/26/2025

To those who have actively participated in their own story of beauty, leaving behind pearls—whether through songs, words, or pictures— to inspire those who would come after.

Thank you.

TABLE OF CONTENTS

Introduction vii

Section One

Chapter 1   Learning the Program 2
Chapter 2   Rules of Mental Engagement 6
Chapter 3   The Most Important Thought 16
Chapter 4   Meet Your Brain 20

Section Two

Chapter 5   Shadows 34
Chapter 6   Trauma 40
Chapter 7   Forgiveness 50
Chapter 8   Fear 58
Chapter 9   Shame 68

Section Three

Chapter 10   Letting in the Light 80

Notes 97

INTRODUCTION

In Dr. Luke's account of the gospel, he begins his book with this preface: "Inasmuch as many have undertaken to compile a narrative of the things that have been accomplished among us... it seemed good to me also... to write..." (Luke 1:1-3 KJV). Though others were writing gospel narratives, Luke felt compelled to write his own account of something that had profoundly impacted him.

The information presented in this book is not new or in any way exhaustive. Still, the topics covered here are becoming acknowledged as extremely relevant for health and healing. So, "it seemed good to me also to write" in my voice and from my perspective about these things that have deeply impacted my life.

This information is not going to truly impact your life in one sitting. You are going to make that happen one decision and one thought at a time. It doesn't happen overnight. Challenging the way you think is hard work, it can be overwhelming and sometimes deeply disturbing. But it is the most rewarding adventure you will ever embark on. The journey of healing and owning your own mind–or as I refer to it, making your mind beautiful–changes everything about the way you see and experience life.

The book is intentionally set up in a journal format. As you read my thoughts, personalize the concepts into your own. Half of the book is reserved for you. Fill in the blank pages with your own story, findings, and resources.

No two minds are the same, and no two journeys are the same. We can learn from each other, but we cannot take on someone else's experience as our own. That's the joy and privilege of life. We get to have our own.

Read the pages slowly. I encourage you not to approach them with a "how to" or a "here are the steps" mentality. Instead, challenge yourself to take the concepts and fill in the gaps with the things that make up the story you are writing.

I did not do justice to all the topics covered in this book. We can only truly apply so much at one time. I tried to be as concise as possible, leaving it to you to add the things that resonate and are relevant for you.

We may quickly forget information we receive from others, but we truly own the information that we gather and test for ourselves. So, take what resonates with you and breeze over what doesn't. Mental maturity is the ability to hear new thoughts and the power to decide whether to accept them or not.

The concepts are simple and repeated several times. Sometimes our brain needs both simplicity and repetition. Your body and mind are so incredibly designed, and when you learn to work with them instead of fighting them, you open yourself up to a new world of possibilities. So here's to magnificent, beautiful minds—yours and mine.

-Jenna

Section One

CHAPTER 1

Learning the Program

Have you ever sat down at your computer to start a project using a program that really wasn't designed for what you were doing? It feels like you are fighting against your computer the whole time because you do not have the right tools for the task. On the other hand, if you took the time to download an application that had the features you needed already built in, you could attempt and complete your task with ease, all because the app possesses the information needed to understand what you are trying to do.

Your brain is a computer—a supercomputer in fact. And much like a computer, your brain needs the correct files and programs to function properly.

By files, I'm referring to experiences and gathered information. When we come to something that seems impossible, it only feels that way because we need a file for it. But the good news is that we are acquiring files all the time.

Programs, however, are the deep rooted belief systems we accept and function from. Many core belief systems are set in place as a child, which is why we must be intentional about updating our programs.

Before we can start creating beauty in our minds, we have to make room in our brain. We do this by organizing and replacing old files and programs that we may not even realize we're functioning from. Another analogy might be that of a garden; in a garden, you have to regularly pull out the weeds and old foliage, and you get to plant, water, and watch new things grow. So it is with our minds.

Keep these two analogies, because we're going to build on them. But

before we move forward, I want to introduce you to eight rules of mental engagement that will be foundationally important to understand in our endeavor. I'll mention them briefly here, and then we'll see them come into play more in the following chapters.

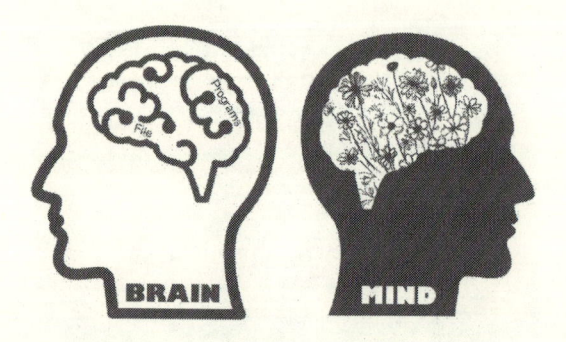

CHAPTER 2

Rules of Mental Engagement

#1 *Thoughts can be changed.*

Everything in life stems from a thought. Behind every action, word, intent, and creation is a thought.

Therefore, before anything can happen or (more importantly) change, there has to be a new thought. Taking time to examine and challenge our own thoughts and beliefs is one of life's greatest hacks. If there is something in your life that is not the way you want it, you have to trace it back to the thoughts that created it. Somewhere along the line there is an old or incorrect thought process—and therefore, an incorrect belief—that has to be changed. But the good news is this: all you're dealing with is a thought, and thoughts can be changed.

#2 *What you focus on will grow.*

If something is bothering you, take away its only power—your attention.

Have you ever felt a sensation in your body and stopped to think about it? A pain in your arm that felt like a pin prick quickly escalates to the pain of a screw driver poke. Almost instantly, you begin feeling like a knife is protruding out of your arm. Suddenly, you notice pain all over your whole body. There can only be one possible explanation for all this unexplained pain: you're probably dying.

While this is an over-exaggerated scenario, you know exactly what

I'm talking about. If you had felt the same pain while in the middle of a work project or when your brain was otherwise occupied, the sensation would have probably lessened if not gone away completely. But because you stopped and focused on it, it grew.

We do this with more than just bodily sensations of course, and this principle of focus can work for or against us.

In Matthew's account of the gospel, we see Jesus explaining it this way: *"The eye is the lamp of the body. So, if your eye is healthy, your whole body will be full of light, but if your eye is bad, your whole body will be full of darkness. If then the light in you is darkness, how great is that darkness"* (Matthew 6:22-23 ESV).

This is very helpful to remember as we work toward healing and creating beauty in our minds. If you focus on the light, it will grow brighter, but if you focus on the unhealthy things that block your light, you will have darkness. Even though the light is there, it can be blocked to the point that all you see and feel is darkness. That's why it's called a great darkness.

What fills your mind will become your reality, so what you choose to focus on is very important.

#3 *You already have all the answers.*

We live in an incredible time of instant information. We can get the answer to anything in a matter of minutes. A quick Google search yields a plethora of sources and opinions at our fingertips. We can find a podcast, blog, YouTube video, or support group for every topic out there. Yet we feel more lost and confused than ever. Why? Because we forgot how to go inside and listen to the part of us that knows the answer.

Jesus said, *"Ask, and it will be given unto you; seek, and you will find; knock, and it will be opened to you"* (Matthew 7:7 ESV). When we think of ask, we often think in terms of physical things like a house or new car. But what if the ask isn't just a request for the physical, but a question? Then, what we would receive wouldn't be a thing but an answer.

This journey is about learning to listen. We have to stop reaching for outside sources to fix us. Although they are important in our life,

sometimes doctors, experts, therapists, friends, or pastors can't give us the answer we need simply because they don't know. Only you do. So learn to quiet your body, slow down your mind, go internal, and just ask. Then expect and wait for an answer. It may come right away, or it may take a little while. Sometimes we're not ready or we're not really wanting to hear the answer yet, and that's ok. Just keep asking, and know the answer is coming. Because if you ask, it will be given. Learn to practice the art of being still. Maybe stillness is a very uncomfortable or unsettling thing for you. If you are that person, I greet and welcome you to the club. Just know, as we go along you'll find that the more you clean out and plant in your garden, the easier it is to enjoy sitting quietly in it. So ask. And if you never stop to listen for an answer, you probably won't get one. Answers come to the quiet, to those listening.

Note: If you're not getting an answer, maybe you need to ask a different question.

#4 *Watch for indicators.*

Computers give us pop-up warning signs, or indicators, when something in the system is not functioning according to design. So does our body. We often call them triggers or symptoms, but I want you to think of them as indicators. Generally, we think of triggers and symptoms as things that need to be stopped or ignored. But if we see them as indicators our body is giving us, we can change the way we handle them.

Indicators are usually preceded by emotions, and if we are not careful, we will focus on the emotion and miss the pop-up sign telling us what is really going on. That's what we want to focus on and address, not the emotion itself. Sometimes indicators can bring painful emotions like fear or shame with them, especially if we respond to them incorrectly. But if we see them simply as indicators, then we can shift from thinking I'm a hopeless case to I see the problem. At that point, we have the choice to make the changes necessary. Unknown problems will never get fixed, and they won't just go away either. So, learn to watch for your indicators. Pay attention, and they will show you exactly where a problem is—where something needs to be healed or removed.

#5 *It's never just one thing.*

A health crisis, mental or physical, generally cannot be attributed to just one thing—one incident, one negative emotion, one anything. It's always going to be deeper than that. Health crises very often involve multiple contributing factors.

Our bodies are miraculous, not to mention incredibly smart. They are equipped with many backup systems that keep us alive. So, if it were just one thing, your body could and would handle it. It's a boss at handling things. When you're working through an issue, just know there are probably layers. One victory or one change may not be enough to make a permanent new pathway for your brain. Healing sometimes requires patience and repeated steps of improvement done over and over again. You cannot give up, get discouraged, or think you are forever broken. Small steps repeated over and over create familiar and well worn pathways for your brain to work with. So if the problem doesn't get fixed the first time, it's not hopeless, it's just more than one thing. Keep going.

#6 *The Power of Agreement*

Thoughts do not have power until you believe or agree with them.

This goes for good and bad thoughts. Becoming a child of God happens through simple agreement. The concepts of the gospel that you must "confess with your mouth and believe in your heart" (Romans 10:9) are only concepts until you believe them, and immediately your position changes. How is it possible that one minute you are a stranger to God and the next his child? That is the power of agreement. You see, others can hear the same concept, but until they come into agreement with it, it holds no changing power for them.

This applies to our thoughts and emotions as well. Let's take fear as an example. Fear has no power where there is no agreement. When you are presented with a thought that has fear attached to it, you have the choice to agree with it and let fear transform you or to see it as only an indicator, use the information and move on.

Negative thoughts and emotions are master intimidators. They try

to make your mind think they are big enough to forcibly take control, but once you retrain your mind to believe you are the one in ultimate authority and refuse to step down, then all you're dealing with is a thought, and thoughts can be changed. Their intimidation becomes less and less overpowering. In essence, you are renewing your mind. You're equipping it with a new program while simultaneously retiring the old default one.

New program: Nothing has power over me unless I give it that privilege.

#7 *It's not too hard. It's not too big.*

When you don't have the right file and well worn mental path of experience in any given situation, your brain is immediately overwhelmed and wants to give up. You know the intimidation and fear you feel when you attempt to do something for the first time? Once you do it, and especially if you do it over and over, you are no longer intimidated by the task. Your brain just needs the right file. So when you're overwhelmed, remind yourself: this is not too hard, and it's not too big. I just need to learn the new file.

#8 *Change can begin at any moment.*

That significant point when everything begins to change can happen at any moment. All it takes is a thought.

Thoughts are the control agents. By simply changing the way you think about your situation–past or present–you can completely change the entire narrative. Although you cannot always immediately change your external circumstance, you can change something more impactful- yourself. Change in any situation, circumstance, or season starts the moment you say it does. All it takes is the thought that says so. Stop and read that again. If all you get from the book is this one point, it was worth the time writing it. Change–your change–starts the moment you decide it does.

CHAPTER 3

The Most Important Thought

Program update: I am in authority. Therefore, I am not a victim. This concept might make you feel upset (as I felt when it was lovingly pointed out to me). It might make you feel like nobody really understands your unique situation. Or it might cause you to think: "That's right, you tell them. I can't stand a victim."

Take either of those responses as an indicator that this might be a section you need to read over a few times, because if one thing is true about victims, it's that we never think we are being one.

Victim- Helpless. Overwhelmed. Resigned to. Stuck. With no power to produce change. Hopeless. A product of someone else's choices.

If we're honest, we've all been here at some point. It can often be so hard to see in ourselves because our brain will not call it what it is. It will always find another name for it. You must intentionally watch for the "victim thought" and call it out. Here's a hint: If you pay attention carefully the next time you want to make an excuse or want to pass blame for what's going on—even if it's 100% logical—you'll probably spot the victim mentality. Immediately ask yourself, "Am I in control, or am I giving that power to someone else?" You will have just a minute to answer before your brain will follow up with a convincing explanation of why it's totally out of your control.

Feeling like a victim is often an irrational instinct driven by fear and attached to what seems to be a very logical excuse. But excuses never leave us empowered. In fact, as long as we're satisfied with our excuses, we will

remain in a cage with an open door, insisting someone or something is keeping us there. We cannot create beauty with a victim mindset. But the great news is this: You are not a victim.

Say it with me—I AM NOT A VICTIM.

I am not a victim to my job, my circumstance, my home, my parents, my past, or my mistakes. I am in authority and have the power to change myself and my mindset at any moment that I choose. The starting point of change can happen at any moment. It is your birthright. You get to have full control over your mind until you choose to give that control to someone or something else. Remember, the fruit of the Spirit is self-control.

Victims play the blame game. Our brain does not want to think ill of itself. Therefore, it either must justify what happened by making an excuse, or it must blame what happened on someone. Both are games that will leave you the loser every time. I know it's offensive and even scary to take responsibility for the outcome of your own life, but I also know the freedom that it brings. It is not until we are sick and tired of playing the victim that we can truly heal and work through our current (or past) situation. Only then can we hope for change in the future.

We are in control of every thought that stays in our heads. We are not in control of the thoughts that pass through, but we get to choose the ones that stay and the ones we interact with. If you will decide today you are taking full responsibility for your own life, no matter what anyone else did or didn't do, you can work through anything. When you decide you are the one in charge, the narrative changes, and endless possibilities are available. You move into a new position; you move into authority.

Authority- the power or right to give orders, make decisions, and enforce obedience.

You may not be a parent, employer, ruler, or president, but you are in authority over a very important district—your mind. You cannot control anyone else, but you can control yourself.

I have a choice.
I get to choose.
I am in authority, therefore, I am not a victim.

CHAPTER 4

Meet Your Brain

We have already compared our brains to supercomputers, but let's get more specific in our definition of the brain and how it works. Simply defined, your brain is an organ. Granted, it is an organ that controls everything. Johns Hopkins defines the brain as *"a complex organ that controls thought, memory, emotion, touch, motor skills, vision, breathing, temperature, hunger, and every process that regulates the body."*[1]

Although it is a complex organ, it is just an organ. It doesn't know right from wrong or reality from the imaginary. Rather, it deduces according to what it takes in, and it observes cause and effect. It has a simple built-in program with one goal: to keep you alive. Everything it does revolves around that goal. Your brain is extremely efficient, and it has spent your whole life creating frameworks (based on your program or belief system) that it functions from to maintain a sense of safety. Automatic responses, which come from these frameworks, are what you physically and mentally do without even thinking. Your brain does not like to be challenged on them, and it feels extremely threatened if you mess with its program.

Your brain strives to create a safe environment for you and will go to extreme measures to protect you from anything that it thinks would cause you harm. Where it cannot physically protect you, it emotionally protects you by pushing emotions and memories (which it either does not know how to handle or does not want to handle) out of the line of consciousness so we remain "safe". When your brain does not have the right files to deal with these unwanted emotions and memories, it simply chooses not to.

Though designed for our protection, this is an often misused function.

At times, our brain and body perceive uncomfortable emotional sensations as dangerous. This is the reason why it is so hard to deal with things that are unpleasant in our life; our brain naturally wants to divert them. Much of how our brain functions originates from fear.

Our brains love the familiar. It feels safe when it can predict and even autopilot through situations. As we move forward, we can see how this plays a huge role in why we feel something is impossible when, in reality, it is very possible. Recognize that the "freaked out" feeling is just your brain navigating through the unknown. Like a strong-willed child, it needs to be instructed, reinforced, and encouraged over and over again. Learning to help our brain is so important because we want our brain working with and not against us. We do that by practicing, reinforcing, and equipping it with files.

Although the brain regulates our bodily processes, it is not actually the one in charge. The brain gets all the attention because it's the physical part we can see, examine, and study. But there is a "behind the scenes" character you need to meet and understand.

Will the real intelligence please take the stage…

Let's Hear It For - Your Mind.

This is the real boss. When they say "it is all in your mind," they aren't joking. Your mind, the sense of consciousness housed in your brain, is the actual controller and regulator. Our brain can send commands to the rest of the body, but our mind understands and determines them. If your brain was a king, your mind would be its most trusted advisor. Said another way, your brain is the vehicle, and your mind is the driver.

There is so much we could say about the mind, and the conclusions are as deep as they are wide. That is not our goal here, but I would encourage you to do some personal study on the mind. In fact, the Bible has a whole lot to say about it.

Just as your brain learns well worn paths and defaults back to them, your mind will also default back to well worn thoughts and conclusions. It is also very efficient.

According to neuro specialist Dr. Caroline Leaf, *"Although your mind*

can move quickly from one thought to another, it can actually only think one thought at a time.²" When you consider all the thoughts flooding your mind, this is amazing; they are really only coming in one at a time. This will become significant later when we are retraining our mind. Remember, when it feels hard, just focus on choosing the right thought, one thought at a time. You can't think a fearful thought at the same time as a peaceful thought.

Am I Getting On Your Nerves?

Your brain communicates with your body via bolts of energy sent rapidly through your nervous system. You are basically a walking electrical power house. Your mind determines the energy and signals the brain through a thought. The brain then sends the message to the body. All of this occurs within milliseconds. But don't miss this: your mind communicates with your brain through a thought, and that thought is the spark that ignites the impulse sent by your brain to your body.

Now, you may be thinking, "thanks for the obvious anatomy lesson," but stay with me. This is so simple, yet it is the basis of everything we are going to talk about in the pages to follow.

Let me quickly recap. Your brain functions out of its natural programming. Beyond our automatic responses, our mind controls everything, and it does so through thoughts.

Wait, so a thought is what controls or changes everything in my body and perception? Yes.

As we said in rule #1, all you're really dealing with is a thought.

But The Plot Thickens…

Thoughts come from our mind, both conscious and subconscious, and they are often influenced by things outside of us. Thoughts can come from social media, movies, books, other people, and even invisible forces, just to name a few.

This is why we must pay attention to the thoughts we allow to run through our head. That may seem like a daunting task, especially since our

culture is both excessively busy and incredibly immersed in entertainment. We can go all day without even noticing the thoughts that are coming across our mind. But that does not make them any less impactful on our bodies. Thoughts are influencers. Every cell in your body responds to every thought you think.

And Now For The Fun Part–

Thoughts can also carry emotions with them.

An emotion is energy in motion: e-motion. Emotions can get a bad rep. They can also be blamed for a lot of bad behavior. But an emotion in its simplest form is energy. It is an energy produced by the brain and sent to the body in reaction to a thought produced by memories, events, experiences, or people, among other things.

Emotion is an energy that we get to choose to interact with. And the emotions that we interact with for long enough become a part of us. The cells in our body respond to the thoughts we think and the emotions we feel. As thoughts and emotions create energy through the body, this energy affects our health. When we are talking about emotions, positive and negative don't just mean good and bad. Positive emotions are those that work with our body's design, while negative emotions work against our body's design. Positive emotions are beneficial to our health, while negative emotions can leave our bodies open to harm.

Research shows that 75 to 98 percent of mental, physical, and bahavioral illness comes from one's thought life.
-Dr. Caroline Leaf[3]

Now, remember our note on authority? Here's where we put it to play. When we are presented with a thought attached to an emotion, we have a split-second choice to decide how we interact with it. Just know that whatever you do, you get to choose. We're not victims, right? Remember, the starting point of change can happen at any moment. At any moment you can choose to step out of that emotion, simply by changing the thought. Simple, but unfortunately not always easy.

So, What Does My Heart Have To Do With It?

Like the brain, there are so many things we could say, but to keep it simple and applicable, here are a few things I want you to remember about the heart. In Proverbs, Solomon says *"Keep thy heart with all diligence, for out of it are the issues of life" (Proverbs 4:23 KJV)*. He was speaking literally of blood, which is our life source, but he was also speaking metaphorically of something deeper when referring to these "issues." Picture your heart as the Grand Central Station to your traveling emotions. They all come through the heart, like a sort of check point station. We talked about how your brain does not want to deal with things it does not have a file for, and if you attempt to do so without a file (or even with a new file for the first time), it will freak out. We want to put our brain in a position where it feels safe so that it is working with us, not against us. We want our heart to be working with us as well. Where the brain in fear will suppress emotions it doesn't want or know how to deal with, the heart in pride will deceive us into thinking they just don't exist at all—one of those "you don't see anything" Houdini numbers. This is the heart's way of accomplishing the same goal as your brain, keeping you alive. *"The heart is deceitful above all things, and desperately sick; who can understand it?" (Jeremiah 17:9 ESV)*. We'll see this come into play more in the upcoming chapters, but the heart's deceitfulness is why we can have a glaringly obvious issue that everyone else can see, while we think we're doing great. Not only do we feel we are doing great, but we are also very agitated by those around us who have the same issue as us. You see, the truth is that your body doesn't want to think poorly of itself. No one wants to live with the true weight of their negative emotions. We function much better when we believe well of ourselves and when we believe that, although deep down we know it's not true, everything is fine.

Our heart has great potential for both love and deception. That's why we are told to keep it. Just as we need to intentionally check every thought we allow our minds to dwell on, we need to take great care in paying attention to the emotions we allow our hearts to interact with.

Remember, emotion is an energy that you get to choose to interact with. The thoughts come from our brain, but the interaction happens in our heart. Healing has to start with getting dangerously honest about who we really are and what's really in our hearts and minds. As long as you are content to fall for the "everything is fine" line, you will never see the need to put in the hard work of uprooting what's really there.

Are You Ready To Heal?

The heart is a master at hiding things. So as we are cleaning out our checkpoint for clear passage, just know this isn't a one and done, quick as a whip process.

You might need to sit in quiet with God and really examine yourself. David prayed, *"Who can discern his errors? Declare me innocent from hidden faults." (Psalm 19:12 ESV)*. It requires the honest desire to know and the patience to look and wait for what may come up.

A life changing piece of advice was given to me when a mentor, in response to my complaint for help, responded, "You need to ask God for a new heart." Irritated, I immediately thought the same thing you would have. "What on earth does that mean? You're not even listening to my situation or the real problem here. What does my heart have to do with it?" I asked for a new heart every day for over a week before I could ask without a wrong attitude. Two weeks later, what was inside started to come out, and for the first time I could see what I was really dealing with. At that point, I had the choice to change it.

The beginning of your journey will be when you choose to stand face to face with the disturbing ugliness of what is really inside and decide you're ready for beauty. The biggest obstacle is going to be honesty. You can't change what you can't see. So again I ask, no matter what comes up, no matter what you must let go of…

Are you ready to heal?

Section Two

CHAPTER 5

Shadows

Removing the blockers.

Carl Jung is credited for popularizing the term shadow self. The shadow self is generally made up of the parts we deem unacceptable about ourselves.[4] These unwanted parts create dark places in our mind and evoke fear. It's a mysterious thing that stays slightly elusive, and yet its presence is known. And what your mind can't clearly see it only guesses at.

Jung called it the shadow self, puritans called it the dark guest[5], God calls it the flesh[6]. Whatever name you associate with it, it's anything that goes against your body's original functioning design.

Shadow: A dark area where rays from a light source are blocked by an object; the product of something blocking or standing in front of the light.

Those things that obstruct our light and that go against our natural design, I'll be referring to as blockers. Behind every shadow is a blocker. A shadow is not a black pit, bottomless hole, or complete darkness. A shadow equals a blockage of light–your light.

Our brain hates shadows because it doesn't have a built-in file to deal with them. In other words, you were not designed to function with them. You have to actually give your brain the file it needs to be able to remove what blocks your light. We all have blockers. Some people have more than others. Some we willingly take on, while some are given to us or even inherited from birth.

In order to cultivate a beautiful mind, we must remove the blockers. In

the following chapters we are going to touch on four in particular, as well as some thoughts on how to remove them. Consider taking the time to sit and identify your own, even beyond these four, and use the principles to work through them as well.

Blockers can and must be removed. However, there are some blockers that will try to claim a legal right to be there. For some, you will need a source greater than your own. We have to go back to our designer. God is not only our Creator, but also our Savior. Christ overcame the power or legal right of darkness over us through his death and (more importantly) his resurrection.

We may have a blocker that feels beyond our own power, but when we come into agreement with Christ's ownership in our lives, God transfers us from the dominion of darkness into the kingdom of his Son (see Colossians 1:13). This means blockers no longer have the legal right to remain unless we say so.

Christ sets us free and then gives us the mental capability to remove the things that cast shadows and make us feel trapped. As we exercise our authority in removing these blockers, we begin to understand, experience, and enjoy that freedom, not to mention the health and healing that comes with it. And all this empowering change happens in our minds.

The Principle of Exchange

We know that thoughts and their associated emotions create energy and movement in our body, but they also take up actual space as well. Therefore, it is very important to fill that space with something different. When you notice a blocker and remove it, that is an enormous victory! The next step is important, because now it's time to retrain your brain to view that space differently.

Sometimes it's hard to know what to put there, but that's where the principle of exchange comes in. "*...to give unto them beauty for ashes, the oil of joy for mourning, the garment of praise for the spirit of heaviness.*" (Isaiah 61:3 KJV).

It can be as simple as this: God, I give you this jealousy. I don't want it anymore. As I release and let go of what I no longer want in my body,

*... the garment of praise for
the spirit of heaviness.*

what would you put in its place? Then, stop, and just listen. What's the first thing that comes to your mind? Does it completely resonate and maybe even surprise you? That's your exchange. Now, every time your mind wants to return to jealousy, immediately choose to go to your exchange. Maybe your word will be peace, or happiness, or confidence. It will be specific to you. You could write it down where you can see it. Maybe find a verse, quote, or song to reinforce and remind your brain until it's an automatic path. Remember to speak (out loud if possible) to yourself while learning your new pathway, just like you would speak to a child being trained.

I do not have to be **overwhelmed**. I'm feeling overwhelmed, but I don't need to anymore. I am **creative**. I can and will find a solution to this problem. As I relax my body, I will be able to better listen for the answer. I am creating the life I want to live. *New program: I do not have to function from a state of overwhelm.*

Using this as an example, flesh it out to be relevant to you. Replace the bold words with your exchange. It may seem silly, but the practice is effective. You have to give your mind a new file to work with, or it will default back to the old one.

CHAPTER 6

Blocker #1: Trauma

A new title.

In his book The Body Keeps Score, Bessel van der Kolk discusses how traumatic memories impact our minds and bodies. According to his findings, traumatic experiences that overwhelm our ability to cope are stored in our body, even if our minds try not to remember them.[7]

We can pretend that it's not there, but meanwhile, trauma will cast a shadow inside of us. Traumatic events violate our programming and lead to destructive emotions. How do you get rid of the thoughts and emotions that trauma creates? I don't think there is one simple answer to this question, but there is a very powerful quote I want you to remember:

> *"If you change the way you look at things, the things you look at change."* -Dr. Wayne Dyer

I want to stop here and make a very important note. I do not suggest or recommend you go back and try to walk through or relive traumatic events. Doing so can give your control to them, and you are no longer in charge. Remember, you are the one in authority, and now you are choosing truth.Choosing truth doesn't change the facts of what happened, but it does change the narrative. It can close the unfinished and unsettled. Because your trauma is specific to you, there isn't a one-size-fits-all plan for moving through it. The goal is to recognize it's there, release the emotions connected with it, and then teach your mind to see it differently. How

that plays out will look different for each of us, but I want to illustrate the process with this story.

There was a girl who possessed an enormous library. This library was her mind, and it contained many books, each representing experiences and information her brain had accumulated over the years. She had a book for every experience in her life. Some she proudly displayed on the front shelves and tables. Others she tucked neatly in the back. But in the corner of her library was a covered box, which contained stories she wished never existed. Every now and then a "trigger" would disturb the lid, and an ugly book would sneak out, bringing with it an ugly dark feeling to her otherwise cheerful room until she could grab it, stuff it back into the box, and close the lid.

As time went on, she unknowingly became a slave to this box. She guarded it without even realizing, always worried one of those books would escape. Try as she might to forget their existence, it was to no avail, for these books had another terrible feature—an unexplainable, practically invisible, yet very present chain that attached her to them. This chain was the kind you tell yourself isn't there, even though you can feel it really is.

One day she sat at her table and decided it was time something was done about her box. She could spend her whole life guarding it and keeping its contents locked inside, or she could claim her authority, choose to no longer be a victim, and figure out what to do with these disturbing books. It was her library after all.

With wobbling knees but a resolved face, she opened the lid and reached for a book. She did not read through the pages, for those kinds of stories can easily overtake you. Instead, standing to her full height and owning her position as master of her library, she did the bravest thing she could do. She turned to the back and began to rewrite the ending. The existing pages were there and could not be removed. They were a part of her story. But she could change one thing: the ending. With a trembling hand, she took the existing pages and gave them a new twist. Instead of closing with, "She lived with the shame and marred image of herself the rest of her life," she added to it, "until she made the choice to live with it no longer."

The more she wrote, the stronger her fingers became. Then a very strange and wonderful thing began to happen. That book and its horrible cover began to transform, and it no longer carried an invisible chain. As she changed the

ending, she changed the whole narrative, and something else changed—the title. No longer The Day I Lost My Identity, it became The Moment My Life Changed.

The book did not disappear, nor did it become beautiful. But the fear and other emotions it brought were gone. It now sits on her shelf, a visible part of her story. Although it is not beautiful, it makes all the books around it full of beauty. Every story that she pulled out of that box and rewrote received a new title and a new place on her shelf, each one exemplifying more beauty in her library.

Eventually her box became empty. No longer needing its protection, she moved it, revealing a window from which warm beams of light filled the room.

As for the ugly books, they are now being loaned to others who share similar stories. Their new names and endings inspire and encourage others to rewrite their own and illuminate the beauty of their library.

What about the librarian? Inspired by her new-found light and no longer worrying about the box, she spends her days regularly acquiring new and exciting books to add to her collection. On occasion, she'll even invite others in to enjoy them with her. She sits and looks at her stories, amazed by how they all seamlessly run together to make up the narrative that is her present reality, and she is deeply grateful.

****

You may think that sounds too simple. Don't mistake simple for easy. Is it always easy? No. But is it simple? Yes. If you are not at the place where you can move through it, it's ok. Ask God to give you a desire for healing that is stronger than the fear of the memory. Your brain is averting it because it wants to keep you safe. But it's not as scary or impossible as it's trying to make you think it is. The moment you decide it will no longer have power over you is the moment you take authority away from the memory.

Be aware that some memories do not immediately change and leave our brains. Some are etched very deeply, and even when given new endings, the old narratives still try to replay in your mind. That doesn't mean they will forever haunt you. It simply means that your brain has to learn to see them differently. Every time an old thought or memory arouses emotion, you must learn to identify it and talk your brain through how you will

remember and see that memory. Again, experiences don't disappear, but they can be renamed. Teaching yourself the new narrative will, in time, completely transform it. For some memories, it happens quickly, and for others it's a gradual relearning process.

Guard your mind; don't allow it to go back and relive any part of a memory you've changed. The old story, ending, and associated emotions are part of a well worn path that your brain may want to default back to. Continue to teach it the new mental path, and it will eventually catch on. You'll know you're making that progress when you think of the situation and your mind goes straight to your new thoughts instead of the old ones.

For the reader that needs to hear it:

Some memories and traumas are not only scary to our brain, but they also can have other things attached to them. Never force your mind to look at something traumatic before you have the proper file to move through it. This doesn't give an excuse to ignore it, but you may need someone to come alongside you and give you some files of truth (think counselor, therapist, pastor, friend, etc). At other times, the file you need can only be found by going to God. You need to ask God for the mental file necessary to deal with it. You may need a power stronger than your own to be able to walk through it. If your memory feels like an unbreakable chain, I have wonderful news for you. Right before Jesus completed his work on the cross and gave up his spirit, he loudly proclaimed, *"It is finished" (John 19:30)*. What was finished? The payment for every evil that would try to haunt us, every mistake or willing hurt we would cause, and the shame and guilt we would feel. In his death, he finished it. Whatever haunts you, visually take it to the foot of the cross and see Christ standing there with the keys of freedom—the freedom that he paid the ultimate price for. There is nothing outside of his reach or beyond his power to forgive and make new. *"But he was pierced for our transgressions; he was crushed for our iniquities; upon him was the chastisement that brought us peace, and with his wounds we are healed." (Isaiah 53:5 ESV).*

I recently heard an amazing story from someone working through a past trauma. Her memories came with tattoos, visible and physical reminders of her experience. After rewriting the end of the story, she started

to research the possibility of having her tattoos (which felt like her scars because of the memories they held) removed. But she heard something inside of her say, "Don't try to remove them. I want you to use them."

It seems like a paradox, but it isn't. When there is freedom, an ugly story can testify of one made beautiful.

CHAPTER 7

Blocker #2: Forgiveness
But how?

Unforgiveness is a tricky thing. Sometimes, we deal with unforgiveness we know is there, but we don't want to deal with. At other times, there is unforgiveness that we are unaware of. Both kinds are extremely destructive and need to be handled as such. When the Bible says you must forgive from the heart (see Matthew 18:35), God isn't making a good Christian suggestion. The instruction is serious, not optional. Our mental and physical health will be directly affected by unforgiveness held in our hearts.

Unforgiveness is an energy—a corroding energy that our bodies were not designed to hold. Given time, unforgiveness will morph into things like resentment and bitterness, which literally weaken our bodies and leave us vulnerable to all sorts of disease.

So how do we get rid of it? Forgiveness is an issue of the heart, not an issue of a person or circumstance. There are people who have suffered unimaginable things and found the freedom of forgiveness, and there are people who have been offended and refuse to claim that freedom.

If you feel you don't struggle in this area, it may be a sign your brain is averting something. So before you breeze past this chapter, genuinely ask God to show you where you may be holding unforgiveness. Who have I not truly forgiven? If you pray that long enough with a sincere and open heart, God will show you. The key is that you must want to hear the answer. Pray as David did in Psalm 139:23-24 ESV: *"Search me, O God, and know my heart! Try me and know my thoughts! And see if there be any grievous way in*

me, and lead me in the way everlasting!" Take some time to truly search, and let God reveal to you if there is any unforgiveness.

Now let's talk about the kind you know is there but don't see how you can let go of. The real question is not can you forgive. The question is: are you ready to heal? One of the hardest steps to healing is being willing to let go and forgive. Proper perspective can be helpful. If you were walking along the street and someone bumped into you, your automatic response might be to push back or get upset. But if you turned and saw the person who bumped you was blind, your perspective on the event would change. Even though you would be jolted, you can have sympathy because the bump was largely influenced by the person's disability.

Hurting people hurt people, and if you can see your offender as broken or obviously suffering from their own hurt, you can foster sympathy instead of resentment. Creating the right perspective is very helpful in letting go and forgiving. It's not excusing or justifying what they did. It's simply recognizing that we are all broken and hurting, and unless you heal, you are capable of causing great pain as well.

When our brain cannot justify forgiveness, it will do a number of things to avoid confronting the problem. It may hide the unforgiveness and pretend it's not there, or it may enlarge it and make you believe it is impossible to let go of. The steps toward forgiveness have to start with your own willingness to agree that the unforgiveness is there and that it cannot stay.

Remind yourself that though your brain feels like this is impossible, it is not. Forgiving this person does not have to do with them or their actions. It has everything to do with you and the beauty you're creating.

When a specific person or circumstance comes to mind that you feel you cannot move past, try this exercise:

Write down everything that you're holding against that person, but start each item with I forgive you for...

I forgive you for taking advantage of my time and money.
I forgive you for not protecting me.
I forgive you for your lies that destroyed my name.
I forgive you for _____ and at the end of your list write down and say out loud:

I forgive you, and you are free. I forgive myself, and I am free.

In some cases, the offense is mutual, and you need to contact that person and apologize for your part in the hurt. Sometimes, you must accept that you will not get an apology from the other person, and you may not receive the gift of verbal closure. But the beauty of wanting to truly heal is that it won't matter if they apologize or not. You can still choose to forgive them—you're doing this for you.

When writing your list, take your time and allow the hurts to come to your mind. Sit with them for a minute and ask yourself (even out loud): "Can I forgive this? Am I ready to heal?" Maybe the answer is no. It's okay. Come to God with honesty and openness. He's not offended by your honesty. Ask him to help you desire healing more than anything else. Ask him to show you how to let this go. If you're not ready, fold your paper and save it for later.

We all have "light bulb" words or concepts that make things click for us. If you are not able to release what you are holding, ask yourself: "What needs to click to help me let go?" The next day, find a quiet place to pull out your paper and ask yourself the same questions. "Can I forgive this? Am I ready to heal?" You may need to do it for several days. You might try repeating, "I forgive you, and I set you free. I forgive myself, and I choose to be free," even before you feel a breakthrough. If it's not true yet, speak it until it is.

When you hit a breakthrough and are ready to let go, roll your list into a torch, take it outside, and burn it. As you watch the paper shrivel and turn to ash, verbally repeat, "I forgive you, and I am free. I am ready to heal." Then look at your little heap of gray ashes and blow them away.

Unfortunately, this is not a ceremony that will magically get rid of your resentment, but it is a physical representation of release that signals our body and mind that we are letting go.

Now think back to the principle of exchange. When you let go of something, you need to replace it with something to take its place. Ask God what you can put in this space, and see what word comes to your mind—maybe joy, laughter, peace, or warmth. Depending on the depth and frequency of the offense, you may be able to release it quickly without it ever coming up again. Deeper hurts may take time and come with frequent

reminders. This is where your exchange comes in. The next time you feel that shadow of unforgiveness moving through your mind, go immediately to your new word. If your word is peace, whenever your mind wants to replay hurts or bring up an old emotion, take control and choose to think thoughts of peace instead. Your brain may catch on right away, or it may need to be trained over and over again. It's not a sign of how strong or weak your brain is, but instead a sign of how deeply the memory affected you. Don't let yourself get discouraged or go into autopilot and start thinking you can not let it go.

You can let it go, and God will help you. Now you just have to go through a process of retraining your brain what to think, which will affect what your heart will feel. Do not get discouraged; the more you do it, the more your brain is learning.

Remember, unforgiveness will deceive you into thinking it has a right to stay, or it will make you think it's impossible to get rid of. Both are lies, and you have to recognize them and replace them with truth.

It's my mind, and I can choose how I think. At all costs, I am ready to heal. My mind is becoming a place of beauty, and there is no place for this here.

Special note:

What if the person you can't forgive is you?

We will come to this again when we discuss shame. But in short, I would encourage you to write it all out and ask the same questions: "Can I forgive this? Am I ready to heal?" You might also ask, "Can I be forgiven for this? Is this possible to heal?" Ask God over and over again until you are ready to hear the answer. I'll give you a hint: the answer is always yes. There is always forgiveness. God offers unconditional love and forgiveness to his children. *"If we confess our sins, he is faithful and just to forgive us our sins and to cleanse us from all unrighteousness." (1 John 1:9 ESV) "...and forgive us our debts, as we also have forgiven our debtors." (Matthew 6:12 ESV).*

God offers us both the blessing of extending forgiveness and the blessing of receiving it. The fact that we have been forgiven gives us the ability to extend forgiveness, even to ourselves.

CHAPTER 8

Blocker #3: Fear

Oh no you won't!

Phrases such as "fear not," "be not afraid," and "let not your heart be troubled" are found all throughout scripture. It's only logical to assume that God gives us these commands over and over again because we would face moments in our lives that would incite fear in us.

Fear hides behind many masks, and if we're not careful, we can call fear other names. But so many of our poor decisions, missed opportunities, and ruined relationships result from fear.

Fear is an emotion stemming from a belief. The Oxford Language Dictionary defines it as "an unpleasant emotion caused by the belief that someone or something is dangerous, likely to cause pain, or a threat."[8] Remember, fear has no power where there is no agreement. We have to identify and then change the belief (the program) that we are functioning out of. Call fear by its name, and don't let it hide.

It is important to identify what exactly it is that we are afraid of, or what the real source of the fear is. Sometimes, our brain will attach the real source of fear to unlikely sources so that we can avoid confronting the actual fear. Take, for example, someone who fears riding in a car that they are not driving. Being in the passenger seat is not the actual fear; the real fear may be giving up control or trusting someone else with their wellbeing.[9]

Take time to try to identify the true source of your fear and not just the unlikely or illogical cover-up. Remember, knowledge dispels fear. If you can name it, you can disempower it. If fear is like a giant holding you

in his fist and saying, "I'm going to eat you!" then confronting fear is being able to look right back at him and say, "Oh no you won't."

You can get to that place of security one choice at a time. For every scary thought that haunts your mind, remind it that you are the one in authority and no thought can stay without your consent. Remember, you can only think one thought at a time. So, you have to carefully select every thought until you walk out of the forest and see the sky again.

The Fear Stomp

In a climactic scene of C.S. Lewis' novel The Silver Chair[10], the young protagonists find themselves trapped by a witch as they attempt to save the prince. The witch throws powder into the fire, and as the room fills with a strange smoke, the witch begins speaking lies in a gentle, sweet voice. At first, the children resist every word, but as she speaks them over and over, their minds become foggy and they start to agree with her words in a trance-like state. Puddleglum, a creature from Narnia, realizes what he is saying and begins to proclaim truth. But as the witch continues to speak, his mind becomes foggy again. It's not until he takes his bare foot and stomps on the fire, cutting the smoke, that everyone breaks from the witch's spell and regains their mental clarity.

This scene powerfully illustrates how fear can overtake us. In the story, though the children tried to resist the lies, they were almost overtaken. You often can't resist, argue, or reason with fear. In fact, the more you reason with it, the stronger it gets, because what you focus on will grow. So the focus has to change.

That is what Puddleglum did in his quick physical action, or stomp–he disrupted the conversation.

Sometimes the stomp is as simple as a deep breath. It's a quick jerk that breaks the smoke and gives you a second to gather your thoughts and carefully choose the next one. The fear your body is feeling is coming from a thought, therefore what you need to replace it with isn't better reasoning but a better feeling. If thoughts evoke emotions, then choose a thought that will produce the emotion you want your body to feel in that moment instead of fear.

Gentle Strength

Sometimes, all you need to do is calmly disengage with the fear. Try this power thought: "If that happens, we'll figure it out." When panic thoughts flood your mind—What if I lose my job? What if my child fails? What if _____?

Instead of continuing down the list of imaginary possibilities, try following it up with "If it happens, we'll figure it out." You've been through tough times and worked through impossible feeling circumstances before. This won't destroy you.[11] Responding to fearful thoughts this way is not carelessness or indifference toward the outcome. It's a mindset of authority that believes that although I may not see the answer, I know there is one. It's calling fear's bluff and refusing to play the game.

Not As Mighty As You Think

My husband and I had the opportunity to go to Maui before the devastating fires in 2023. As we were in the ocean one late afternoon, the waves were the biggest I had ever seen. As they made their way to shore and crashed loudly against the sand, the water under your feet would sweep you toward the next wave with so much force that you had no choice but to be carried into it. If you tried to turn and swim away, you would be picked up by the wave and smashed to the shore. But if you swam towards the wave as it rushed forward, you simply had to jump, and it would roll right under you to the shore. As we jumped one massive wave after another, a file was etched in my mind: Don't turn and run. Swim right into it, face it head on. Just when you think it's going to overtake you, jump. All the might and power of the waves moved effortlessly past me. The mighty waves no longer seemed so terrifying, and with each jump I felt more confident. So it is with fear. The more you face it, the less powerful it will feel.

A note to whom it may concern:

Forcing your brain to face a fear it doesn't have a file for can be dangerous, and if you don't understand when to jump, the wave of fear may very well crash you into the shore. This is where you must learn to

listen. Ask God when to jump and what to think of your fear. Sometimes, facing fear is not a matter of bravery but a matter of quieting your mind to listen for the next step. If you let the emotion of fear fill you, you'll lose the ability to hear the way out. Learn to find that inner light in the midst of the darkness, because darkness has no power over those who hold light.

If you have a long standing fear in your life, or if you identify as a fearful person, you have to know that retraining your brain to handle fear is a continual and reoccurring practice. Again, fear takes on so many different faces, and your brain constantly needs new files to address different fears. But again, as your brain acquires new files and establishes new programs, it will get better at handling fear. You'll have times when you feel fearless, and then something new will come up. You'll have to walk through the process again, one thought at a time. But never get discouraged; your brain is learning, and you are growing. Keep speaking truth to the fearful thought until it clicks, and you find yourself looking the giant right in the eye and hearing your own voice say, "Oh no you won't."

Stepping Out of Your Comfort Zone

One proactive thing we can do to deal with fear is intentionally stepping out of our comfort zone. We all have our comfort zones–places of supposed security that make our brains feel safe. Stepping out of that comfort zone causes your brain to panic. Activities outside of our comfort zones might be signing up for a singing audition, giving a public speech, having a hard conversation, or inviting a new person over to your home. When you do those daunting or scary things and live to tell about it, your brain observes the outcome, creates a file and enjoys a boost of dopamine for the accomplishment. If you repeatedly give speeches in front of an audience, your brain will catch on and no longer view public speaking as life-threatening. You may even enjoy it and begin to look forward to it. Why? Because your brain now has a file for public speaking and sufficient practice using it. It no longer feels threatened by that activity.

Regularly stepping out of our comfort zone can be very beneficial

in helping our brains learn to deal with fear. When you find yourself struggling in a fear cycle (in which all of your decisions are being made from a place of fear), challenge yourself to do something that makes you feel uneasy. We are designed to do hard, amazing, and creative things. Don't let fear cripple you from living up to that potential.

CHAPTER 9

Blocker #4: Shame

That's not my name.

The first recorded instance of shame is found in Genesis three. Adam and Eve had willingly disobeyed God by giving into the temptation of the serpent. Immediately following their disobedience, everything changed:

> *Then the eyes of both were opened, and they knew that they were naked. And they sewed fig leaves together and made themselves loincloths. And they heard the sound of the LORD God walking in the garden in the cool of the day, and the man and his wife hid themselves from the presence of the LORD God among the trees of the garden. But the LORD God called to the man and said to him, "Where are you?" And he said, "I heard the sound of you in the garden, and I was afraid, because I was naked, and I hid myself." He said, "Who told you that you were naked? (Genesis 3:7-11 ESV)*

The serpent who had tempted them, saying, "You shall not surely die," very likely turned around and accused: "You are no longer acceptable. Look at you, you're naked! How could God love you?"

That day in the garden, far more happened than just realizing their nakedness. That day, Adam's mind received a file he was not designed to handle. For the first time, he interacted with shame, and it made him hide from his Maker.

Consider Adam's explanation for hiding: "I was afraid, because I

was naked." Why did Adam not think: Wait a minute, I was naked when I walked with God yesterday. In fact, I've looked exactly this way since the day he created me, and he's never said anything about it being unacceptable?

Why wasn't Adam's response to meet with God and explain exactly what had happened, trusting God would know what to do about it? He didn't for the same reason you and I don't immediately go to Him. When Jesus is your Lord and God is your Father, every part of you is covered and acceptable because of what Christ accomplished through his death on the cross. We have access to God Almighty through an identity that is not our own, but Christ's. Yet we still want to hide.

We believe the lie that our "nakedness" makes us unacceptable, when the truth is that we were naked yesterday when God walked with us. God, who knows the beginning from the end, the entire narrative of your life, already knew of today's sin when he loved and fellowshipped with you yesterday. Why? Because our sin has been covered. *"There is therefore now no condemnation to them that are in Christ Jesus." (Romans 8:1 ESV)* The problem is when we choose shame. Satan knows that shame will make you hide, it will change the way you see yourself and once your sense of identity is distorted, his mission is accomplished.

Was Adam really hiding from God because he was naked? No. He was hiding because he did something for the first time that was not in his genetic program. He disobeyed, and in doing so he left himself vulnerable to Satan, who implanted a very destructive file. The damage done that day was certainly physical, but deeper damage was done psychologically. Adam and Eve's mental and emotional ability to experience God was distorted. After that moment, they would never be able to trust God the same way again—to feel the innocence, love, and acceptance natural to their perfect design. It was the first malfunction in humanity.

In its truest form, sin is anything that works against your body's original design. This can be an altering point of view for those who see God as a task master, ready to punish us when we fail to do the right thing. Instead of feeling anger and disapproval from God, feel the compassion of your creator who knows you personally. He knows that what you are choosing is not going to bring you the happiness you think, and the natural consequences that it will bring.

A natural consequence of sin is guilt. Guilt and shame are not the same thing, although they are often used in the same sentence. Guilt is usually a legitimate feeling in response to an action, but shame is a lie we entertain until it becomes a part of who we are. Shame is not just a blocker. It acts like a virus. It does not sit passively; it actively works to deconstruct the foundation of who we are. Once Satan implants shame, our brains learn that pathway and response.

Dealing with Guilt and Shame

So how do we become free of shame? Forgiveness is the file that overrides guilt. And the file that overrides shame? Restoration.

> *"Therefore, if anyone is in Christ, he is a new creation. The old has passed away; behold, the new has come."* (2 Corinthians 5:17 ESV)

Before your mind can truly deal with shame, you have to walk through your own story of forgiveness and restoration. If you haven't yet, maybe that is why you cannot find freedom. Come to Christ honestly. Bring it all to him. Lay it at his feet and then look up at his hands and find the forgivness and restoration he gave his life to purchase for you. Nothing is outside of his power to forgive and make new. In fact, broken things are his specialty.

If you have found forgiveness and restoration and are still choosing shame (because we get to choose), then it's time for a new program: *I no longer allow shame to mar my identity. I do not agree with it. I choose to believe that I am forgiven, restored, and enough.*

Ask God to show you Heaven's perspective of who you are. Ask him to enlarge your capacity to understand how much he loves you, how he not only loves but enjoys you. Ask him to teach you your new name (Matthew 16:18). Then sit and think about what you want to see when you think about yourself. In light of how Christ sees you, what does that physically look like to you? Replace your old program with a new updated true one.

Your brain has to understand and believe your new identity, and your mind has to become so familiar with it that when presented with

condemnation, or when your mind tries to go back to old thoughts about who you were, you can respond without hesitation: **"that's not my name."**

Broken.
Screw Up.
Addict.
Trash.
Mistake.
Failure.

Whatever the word is that tries to lay a claim on you, you have the God-given power and authority to respond back, *"that's not my name."*

The opposite of a shameful identity is a restored identity—that's what true mental healing is all about.

To What End?

Identity.

Hi. My name is Jenna. Who are you?

Your identity is the most foundational thing you possess. Everything in life builds from who or what you believe yourself to be.

A beautiful girl can hear and choose to believe the voice that says she is ugly. It won't matter how the world sees her, because she will always believe herself to be less than. That is her reality, although it isn't true.

A man may be extremely capable, but if he believes he's unable or undeserving, he will never pursue a career or passion that he believes is not accessible to him. Incapability will be his reality, although it isn't true.

A boy with a disability can believe his body is capable of great things and go on to win a marathon, because he refuses to give power to a lie about what he can't do.

In all three cases, it's a simple matter of identity.

If taking authority of your mind is so difficult and uncomfortable, why do it? Why not go on coping, believing the heart's cry that everything is fine? The answer is simple. Identity. Humans in every generation must face the same questions: Who am I? Why am I here? Why do I do the things I do? Yet the answers seem so elusive, and we often live with a distorted perception of reality. Without identity, we lose our purpose.

When you own your mind, you understand your own identity. The lies no longer stick to you. The fear no longer cripples you. The shame no longer calls you. You know your name, and you are proud of it. This doesn't mean you never face these menaces again, but it means that when you do, your brain understands how to move through them. This process is about more than just clearing things out. It's about restoring the person you were created to be.

Understand this isn't a quick and easy transition. It takes time and reinforcement. For some it will be the hardest program you have to replace. But you have the ability to change the way you percieve and what you believe about anything, including yourself.

Section Three

CHAPTER 10

Letting in the Light
Keeping Your Mind. Guarding Your Heart.

I wish I could say that after walking through this book, you will never have to deal with disturbing and unwanted thoughts and emotions again. Even if I did, you would know it wasn't true. These come with the continuing journey and privilege of life. Our goal shouldn't be avoiding them, but seeing them as vehicles to becoming better versions of ourselves. The Bible calls this process sanctification. Remember, ignored emotions and memories do not just disappear. They must be dealt with. When we can reframe our mindset to be informed instead of intimidated by them, we reach a new level of understanding of our own authority.

Become familiar with saying "I don't accept that" and "I don't agree with that" when dealing with your own thoughts. Every time an unwanted thought or emotion comes up, you can shut it down immediately by refusing to give it any importance.

The sooner you do it, the easier it is. Don't let a negative thought gain momentum. Also, know that they can be very persistent; you may have to say no once, then turn around to say no again. Say it and move on in your mind. Don't give it any more attention. Instead, turn your mind to your exchange thought. If you don't have one yet, you can always default to gratitude. This is a great exchange because gratitude is excellent for dispelling negative thoughts.

If you are in a situation and you're struggling for the right thought, borrow one. This is where outside sources become very beneficial. Play a song. Put on a podcast or short by an inspiring speaker. Call or text a

friend. We can't depend on people or things to fix us, but we were not designed to make this journey alone. God has given us each other to share resources and to help one another. When outside sources are viewed properly, they are invaluable.

Important Note:

Sometimes, you will struggle the hardest just before your greatest breakthrough. Picture your brain as a child kicking up the biggest fit right before he gives up. There could be a spiritual aspect to the struggle as well, and you could be fighting more than just your own thoughts. If you start to think you'll never get victory, pay attention. When it feels the hardest, the most hopeless, the most discouraging, I want you to remember this: *That is exactly what the verge of breakthrough feels like.* Do not give up; you are a lot closer than you think.

We were not designed to make this journey alone.

Your Beauty Manifesto:
Creating the new and making it true.

Remember our Principle of Exchange—when something is removed, another thing needs to take its place. We have talked about removing the things that block our light, and now it's time to fill their place with things that thrive in and magnify it. Part of restoring your identity is planting seeds of beauty to fill the space your blockers once held.

So learn to let in the light and allow yourself to bloom. It's time to start planting seeds!

Seeds of Love-

In Chapter 4, we discussed how the energy or electrical movement in our body is affected by our thoughts and emotions. The most healing emotion we can have is love. That is because God is love. When we receive and give love, our body responds in an incredible way. The ability to feel and extend love is one of the greatest gifts in life. Love reflects and magnifies light. If you have experienced a distorted or twisted version of love, ask God to show you what real love looks like. Ask Him what it means to love unconditionally. Consider if your idea of love is tainted with selfishness, conditions, expectations, or motives. Ask Him to show you what his love feels like. Love cannot be taught; it must be experienced to be understood. Practice feeling love, feeling loved, and feeling loveable. You were created with the capability for all three.

Seeds Of Gratefulness-

You can live in a mansion and feel like a pauper or live in a hut and feel like a king. The difference is gratitude. We all have things we'd like to change in ourselves, our homes, our jobs, our family, etc–but the ability to look around and feel gratitude for everything you see is a valuable skill. Try walking around your home and taking time to express gratitude for everything you see. It's so easy to fall into the trap of "not enough," but it only creates gloomy clouds. You can quickly break that cycle by replacing the thought with one of gratitude. Remember our rule on focus; it applies here as well. The more you look for things to be thankful for, the more things you will begin to find. So when you're feeling down, stop and take

a second to truly appreciate everything around you. If you look for the good things, you will find them, because there is always something to be grateful for.

Seeds Of Words-

Words have incredible power. God created the whole world with his words. And yet, we speak them very carelessly. Start taking inventory of the words you say and the way you express things. Speaking words of life, like joy and appreciation, fertilize your garden. Choose to be very intentional about every word you speak and see how it shifts things, not only in your mind, but in the people around you as well. Give your words as gifts; don't throw them as stones. If speaking negatively (especially about yourself) is a struggle for you, try ending every statement with "… and that's just the way I want it." It will help you quickly gauge if you are speaking words of life or destruction. You may want to rephrase what you are expressing. Speak the positive. Speak the good. Speak the beautiful.

Seeds Of Music-

Music is a healing, powerful gift that speaks the language of the soul. It's an effective tool when you need an energy shift. The right song can snap you out of the blues, pick up your spirit when you're feeling overwhelmed, redirect your focus, dispel fear, and much more, all by shifting your mind and vibration. If you're struggling with the right state of mind, don't forget this extremely helpful resource. Thanks to things like YouTube and Spotify, it's so easy to find any song in any category. Find songs with lyrics that call to mind thoughts of thanksgiving, praise, happiness, victory, and so on. Or look for instrumentals like the harp or piano which have a strong healing effect. Music is a gift from God. Use it.

Seeds Of Creativity-

We are products of a designer who loves to create–a God who put order and beauty throughout creation. Whether it's a sunset, a mountain range, or ocean waves, the list goes on and on. He created beauty for us to enjoy and to be inspired by. That creator gene is imprinted inside us, and it is expressed differently in each of us. We are all creative in a variety of ways. Maybe you love to cook delicious meals, arrange music and lyrics, create

videos, paint, write, dance, build, remodel...whatever! We all have things inside of us intended to make this world a better, more beautiful place. Blockers suffocate our creativity, but light and joy ignite it. Take some time to think about what makes you come alive inside.

I once heard a tragic quote that said, *"The greatest paintings aren't in museums, but in graveyards."* They were held in the minds of creative people who never took the time to manifest it for the world to see. What gift did God put uniquely in you? Don't keep it inside to yourself. Share your beauty.

Seeds of New Experiences-

Nothing will give your brain new files like a new experience. We are a collection of our experiences. Get out of your routine and do something totally different. Since there is so much to enjoy and feel in life, don't let yourself only function out of habit. Go. Do. Give your brain some new, fun files to work from. Everyone's definition of fun will differ, but it can be as extravagant as traveling internationally or as simple as trying a new restaurant. Take that class, explore that hobby, learn that skill, visit a luxury spa, or tour a mansion. Rent a kayak, camp outdoors, join a reading club, or get on a debate team. What makes you smile when you think about it? That–go do that. I'm not encouraging you to be reckless or selfish, and no, not every day requires a new experience. Be realistic with what you have to work with. But if the excuse for putting it off is time, you need a new excuse. That one is always holding people back–people of all ages, in all generations, during all seasons of life. We don't find time, we make it. Growing means letting in the sun–the good, the happy, the fun. When was the last time you did something for the first time? While you're focusing on the beauty inside, remind yourself that there are so many good and wonderful things outside.

Seeds Of Self Care-

I'm not just talking about a quiet cup of coffee, spa service, or a day at the beach. (Although we need those too!) I'm talking about taking care of your body–the physical thing you walk around in. It is the most valuable thing you own and the state of it is a determining factor for a lot of opportunities in life. Our physical health directly affects our mental

health, so taking care of our body is a big part of cultivating a beautiful mind. There are a lot of resources and opinions on this topic and it can get complicated to think through all the ways to care for your body. But try to keep it simple. Here's a great place to start:

✺ Get enough sleep. Beauty sleep is not just for your body, but for your mind as well. Sometimes our mental overwhelm would be completely manageable if we just took a nap. Recognize when you are not well rested and make the changes necessary to accommodate your body to get some sleep. It's a miracle worker!

✺ Practice good nutrition. We all have different nutritional needs, but a good start is to eat real food and drink plenty of water. Interestingly, your body can put together its own diet plan. If you cut out the fake, packaged food with lots of sugar and chemicals that make you want more of it, your taste buds will change. You will start enjoying the taste of real food, and the ones you enjoy will be an indicator of your personal nutritional needs. If you really enjoy meat, you might need more protein. If you are loving blueberries, your body may need more antioxidants. The foods you enjoy will shift based on what your body needs. It's not as hard as it seems! It's a mental shift from complicated to intuitional. If you make 80% of your diet real food and pay attention to the ones you enjoy, it will make an enormous difference. And then you can build from there.

✺ Change the way you look at exercise. Your body was made for movement. And as they say, what you don't use, you lose. We all know our bodies need exercise, but sometimes we have distorted attitudes towards it. Exercise does not mean strenuous, hour-long gym workouts (although it can if that's your thing). It does not mean pain, swelling, and an achy back for days. Exercise can be as simple as a walk. In fact, walking is one of the most effective exercises for emotional regulation. There are so many creative and fun ways to incorporate exercise into a sedentary lifestyle. Branch out and try some new ways of moving your body, then see what is most enjoyable to you. Get your heart beating and your blood moving, and you won't believe the mental momentum it will bring!

Seeds Of Outward Reflection-

As you create order in your mind, you'll want to reflect it in your space. If your home, car, or bag were a reflection of your mental state, would it be an accurate one? One of the best accelerators of transformation is creating unity between our private and public worlds. If cleaning your house seems daunting, try cleaning your car, or maybe just your desk. Our outward state is often an indicator of our inward state. Let your mind see a physical representation of what is happening inside.

Not the End, Simply the Beginning

If there isn't anyone in your life telling you that you are doing a great job, I want you to know that I'm shouting it, and I mean it with all my heart. Taking responsibility for your mind and healing from your past is daunting. There will always be another blocker to remove, a new file to acquire, or a situation to work through. But every now and then, don't forget to stop and look at what you have created, how far you have come, and how different your mind looks now. Give yourself credit, for yours is the story of

a mind made beautiful.

Finally, brothers, whatever is
true, whatever is honorable,
whatever is just, whatever
is pure, whatever is lovely,
whatever is commendable, if
there is any excellence, if there
is anything worthy of praise,
think about these things.

-Philippians 4:8 ESV

NOTES

[1] *Brain Anatomy and How the Brain Works.* (Blog) 2024 https://www.hopkinsmedicine.org/health/conditions-and-diseases/anatomy-of-the-brian

[2/3] Dr. Caroline Leaf, *Switch On Your Brain: The Key to Peak Happiness, Thinking, Health* (Baker Publishing Group, 2005)

[4] Carl Jung, *Aion: Research Into the Phonomology of the Self* (Princeton University Press, 1979)

[5] *The Valley of Vision: A Collection of Purian Prayers and Devations* (The Banner of Truth Trust, 1988)

[6] *The Bible* (ex. Romans 13:14, Matthew 26:41, Romans 8:6, Galations 5:17)

[7] Bessel Van Der Kolk, *The Body Keeps Score* (Penguin Books, 2015)

[8] *Oxford Language Dictionary* (Oxford University Press, 1884)

[9/11] Thoughts adapted from *The Mountain is You: Transform Self-Sabotage Into Self-Mastery*, Brianna West (Thought Catalog Books, 2020)

[10] C. S. Lewis, *The Silver Chair* (Geoffrey Bles 1953)

Made in the USA
Columbia, SC
30 April 2025